To those who unknowingly saved me from my monster.

Preface

The past is where you learned. The future is where you apply the lessons. Don't give up in the middle. —Unknown

I was born on October 29th, 1999, to an immensely loving home with two doting parents. I am an only child but always had a fur-sibling by my side. I have always felt a connection to animals, maybe it is because I prefer having an unspoken bond than actually having to speak words. I often feel that being able to communicate in silence creates more of an emotional connection than words ever could. Due to my quiet nature, I am most definitely an introvert. Being around people for long periods of time takes a lot out of me and I truly need a solid chunk of the day to be completely alone. When I come home from a sleepover with friends, for example, I am always in the worst mood. I snap at every question I get from my parents. Twenty-four plus hours around other humans makes me hate humanity for a bit, but really, it's nothing personal.

All of my life, I have felt like an old soul, consistently acting far beyond my years. I often wonder if it is because I am an only child and have always grown up around people who are older than I am, but who can really be certain. Being eighteen, most people I know are trying new things, going to parties every weekend, doing all the stupid things most teens do before college. But me? I think it's all overrated. I'd much prefer hanging on the back deck with my parents and boyfriend rather than go to party with a million people I don't know and will most likely never see again. Although this can be a good trait to have, this maturity makes me feel distant from people my age so I feel like more of an outcast. It is just so much easier for me to carry on a conversation with someone who is twice my age. I felt this way as a kid too; two of my closest friends were at least two years older than me.

My grandfather, Warren, played a big role in my life. He passed away in 2008, however not a day goes by that he doesn't cross my mind. I often think to myself, "I wish Warren were here to see this" or "I cannot imagine the jokes that Warren would make right now." The first house I remember living in had an in-law apartment where my Nana and Warren lived. Many of my childhood memories are with Warren. Whether I was sitting on his back playing "pony," eating junk food, or just watching a tv show, Warren was my best friend. He used to push me in my stroller every morning to the neighborhood general store for his paper and my lollipop. I could be so silly with Warren; completely myself. I was always laughing or smiling extra big in pictures we have together. I often feel that when Warren died, a large piece of me died too, and that was when the anxiety came in to fill the void.

Chapter 1

The flower doesn't dream of the bee. It blossoms and the bee comes. —Mark Nepo

3:01 pm.

My mom rushes me through the front doors of Atlantic Gymnastics and I look out the viewing room window to my class sitting in a circle preparing for warm-ups.

"I'm not going in there."

"Grace, you have to." My mom replied.

"Nope, we are late, I will not go in late."

Gymnastics, school, birthday parties, no matter what it was, I refused to show up late. That moment when everyone stops and turns to look at you makes me

7

feel sick. As a six-year-old in gymnastics, I would watch everyone come in before I would join in, and if I did not get there early, I would refuse to participate. I am an observer, always have been, always will be.

A lot of people would agree, no one likes that moment when all eyes are on you because you showed up late; but for me, this wasn't just an uncomfortable situation, it was like I was under a burning spotlight, being slowly choked to death by my own hands. I always felt that something about me was different and maybe what was one person's uncomfortable situation was my pure terror.

***

The teacher would call on other students and they could whip up an answer without hesitation. But me? I would freeze. All I could think of was how to get my heart to stop feeling like a volcano about to erupt. When I could finally squeeze out an almost inaudible "I don't know," and when the eyes would turn away from me, my face would start to come back to a slightly less tomato color and my hands would turn to tremors instead of earthquakes.

That was the reality of my everyday. I feared failure, I feared not being good enough, and I feared rejection. However, school is not the only place to harbor my fears. This anxiety takes over when anything about a situation is uncertain — when I cannot fully prepare myself for what is going to happen or what could happen.

I have panic attacks when I have to wait for a table outside of the coffee shop.

I have panic attacks walking through a restaurant to get to my table.

I have panic attacks driving somewhere new.

I have panic attacks walking into a room to meet a

group of people for the first time.

Doing anything when there are other people nearby and

when there is a chance someone could be looking at me

makes me feel like I am slowly being pushed into a

smaller and smaller box; like slow suffocation.

Chapter 2

Fear is only as deep as the mind allows.
—Japanese Proverb

Looking back, I always showed signs of my anxieties.

I have not had a birthday party since I was five years old; and that was my first and only one. Well, family and close friends would come over for a bouncy house in our driveway or for a hayride at the orchard but my first real birthday party that I asked for was my one and only. Since I love animals I obviously wanted my birthday to be at the SPCA. I had my own private room filled with animals that my friends and I could play with after we ate cake and did birthday party things. It was safe to say that I was miserable. About halfway through the party, about ten minutes after I named a cat "Princess," I asked my mom if we could leave yet. My parents told me I couldn't leave because it was my own party. I hated being the center of attention and I was ready to be alone. After that experience, I told my parents I never wanted a birthday party again. Spending my birthdays with my parents is way cooler anyway.

When I was in second grade, I was very sick. I was taken to doctor after doctor, and no one could figure out what was wrong with me; I kept throwing up, I would get these awful stomach aches, I spent a week in the hospital. The more that I think about this time period, I think it was all stress. I would work myself up to the point of illness. This is why no one knew what was wrong with me, it was all in my head.

As a young kid, I did not have too much of a problem going to preschool or kindergarten everyday. However, all of a sudden in the middle of first grade, my mom struggled with getting me to go on the bus. I would start to go up the three steep steps of the bus but then just turn and run back to my mom. I also remember pretending to be sick a few times so that I could miss a day of school. Warren died the year I was in first grade and I am now realizing that I showed all the signs of anxiety, I just never understood what it meant.

***

I would put up quite the fight on Sunday mornings when my mom told me it was time for Sunday School at church. I had already gone through an entire week of school and I was not about to spend a few hours with complete strangers. No matter how hard she tried, I would kick and scream and refuse to leave the house. My mom took this as a revolt against church itself but it was really just against the people that I would be surrounded by. I mentally could not handle the feelings that came with being around people any longer after an entire week of school, especially to be around strangers.

I had God in my heart, however, and found faith on my own. I used an online list of proverbs that relates to certain feelings I was experiencing. I found a lot of hope in these proverbs. For example, if I was feeling afraid, I read Joshua 1: 9, "Have I not commanded you be strong and courageous, do not be afraid or discouraged for the Lord your God will be with you." If I was feeling depressed, I read Psalm 34: 18, "The Lord is close to the brokenhearted and saves those who are

crushed in spirit."

Chapter 3

All she wanted was for someone to look

at her and see the person she hid so well.

—Atticus

I remember every moment I said something I wish I could shove back into my mouth or did something that made me wish I were invisible. I remember getting in trouble for the first time in Mrs. Young's first grade class because Steve made me laugh and I "disrupted" the class. I remember "circle time" in fifth grade, sharing about a riding competition where I came in second place and Joe laughed at me and asked why I didn't win. I remember throwing up on Mira walking through the hall from French class in second grade. (She still won't let me live that one down). I remember tripping on the rug and face-planting in the hallway in fourth grade and having to get up as my entire class laughed at me. I remember getting the easiest question wrong in my 7th grade math class. I remember passing out in front of the entire culinary class on the first day of my sophomore year, knocking over a cart of utensils in the process. I remember failing my driver's test and sobbing in the car in front of the officer. I remember tripping over my backpack in Mrs. Nelson's Sophomore Biology class when I was passing in my exam, falling on my face and flipping a desk.

I remember each of these moments so vividly that it almost feels like they happen all over again when I think about them. I can bring myself back to the exact moment, feel every emotion, see every detail of the setting, and feel completely paralyzed. These moments run over and over in my mind, haunting me; a constant reminder of being imperfect. I am a perfectionist so accepting imperfection is nearly impossible.

***

Being in the spotlight in front of my peers scared me to my very core. I could not even ask a question without my hands trembling and feeling sweat rolling down my sides. One time in 9th grade I was on a double date at the mall. I ended up starving myself because I did not want to order in front of everyone. Thinking back, I am embarrassed by my actions. I live in a small town and I had about 50 kids in my middle school class. Everyone knew everyone. I still felt shy around my classmates even though I had grown-up with them. Middle school was certainly tough but I managed to keep the worrying to a minimum and the fear did not control me. However, high school was a shock to my system, and freshman year was when I fell apart.

FRESHMAN YEAR

Chapter 4

Worry never robs tomorrow of its

sorrow, it only saps today of its joy.

— Leo Buscaglia

"Okay everyone, arrange yourself into a circle. Now say your name, something about you, and then repeat the name of the person next to you."

"Hi, I'm Alyssa and I like to ski and Alex is next to me."

"Hi, I'm Max and I like to play soccer…" The voices would start to become background noise to all the panic in my brain. *WHAT IS MY NAME?!? Oh gosh, I forgot my own name…* My mind would be completely blank to just about everything I've ever enjoyed and even what my name is.

Oh no, my turn.

"Hi, uh, I'm Grace, and, uh, I like to run and, um, Sophie is next to me." *I mumbled way too fast. But whew, I did it. I spoke in front of people and remembered my name. But running? I like to run? Grace what were you thinking, when was the last time you even put on running sneakers?*

Ask just about anyone and they will tell you that they hate icebreakers. Standing in a circle with a bunch of strangers having to say your name, one thing about you, then recite the person's name next to you, was not my idea of a good time. I would never even remember anyone's names because I was so stressed out about having to say something about me.

The first day of freshman year was an entire day of icebreaker activities, so clearly, high school was already off to a bad start.

My high school used block scheduling and I happened to have a split first block. This means that I had the same two classes for forty-five minutes for the entire year in addition to three other blocks that are 90 minutes long. My split block consisted of Freshman English and French II. Out of all the classes that I had my entire year, these two led to an immense amount of stress.

My freshman English class will haunt me forever because that was my breaking point. The teacher had this cruel idea of randomly calling on a student to read their personal essay or journal entry

23

aloud. He would make us go up in front of the class, read an excerpt from Julius Caesar that we had never seen before and analyze it. I would spend hours on homework that would take any other kid twenty minutes to complete. I had to ensure that every answer was correct and in-depth because I was so worried that he was going to call on me to read my answers the next day.

The idea of going to that class everyday made me dread waking up in the morning. I would go to sleep as early as possible just so the anxious feelings would stop. Walking towards that classroom, the hallway would become seemingly darker and the walls seemed to cave in on me. My legs would feel like cement and my heart would be racing so fast I would feel like I could not breathe. Some days, I would even have the illusion that I was going to throw up.

Little did I know, this was just my irrational fear at work.

***

French class was a whole other story. Imagine English class, but in a foreign language. Yeah, talk about a disaster. Madame and I got off on the wrong foot to begin with because she expected students to actively participate in class and at that point, participation was no longer in my vocabulary.

There was no way in hell that I was going to raise my hand or willingly answer a question in French, I struggled enough with speaking aloud in English.

Between the oral assessments and skits, my anxiety levels could not have gotten any higher. I was waking up every day knowing I was going to have to speak in front of the class one way or another. A fear that I had been able to manage my entire life, was now completely out of hand.

Many nights I found myself in tears when I did not understand the French work. I was too scared to ask for help so I was left to figure it out for myself, which did not work so well. I truly did not understand what we were learning at times and this meant that when I did get called on, I would have no idea what to say and this caused even more anxiety.

***

The anxiety that came with everyday became unbearable. It got to the point where I knew that if I did not get help, I would be in a very dark place. Before I got my driver's license, my mom and I would spend an hour driving back and forth to the horse barn where I rode almost everyday. I had been telling her how much I hated going to school but she would always retort with a positive spin on what I was feeling and say I was just going through a big adjustment from such a small school before. One ride, I decided to tell my mom how bad it really was, how I wasn't sure I could stand it much longer, but the hardest part was that she truly did not understand. I would tell her how certain situations were making me feel and she would tell me to just get over it. Well, if it were that simple, I wouldn't have even asked for her help.

Chapter 5

Sanity and happiness are an impossible

combination. —Mark Twain

The hardest part for me was admitting that I needed help. I had always taken pride in my ability to be independent so accepting that I could not do this by myself was a really hard pill for me to swallow. My first thought was to convince my parents to let me drop out of school and enroll in an online school. Let's just say, that did not go over so well. For two successful adults who did not understand what I was going through, they did not think twice about this proposal being a cry for help.

Although, I eventually learned that I was not so different from my dad. He too experienced a form of social anxiety however he just sucked it up and got through school, so that was his advice for me.

"I did it, you can too."

But that just isn't how I function. As a family, we continued to discuss my anxieties about school and came to the conclusion of getting professional help.

Chapter 6

The happiness of your life depends on the quality of your thoughts. —Marcus Aurelius

Walking through the large glass doors into the lobby, I was slapped in the face with that sterile smell that reminds me of dying. I scanned the waiting room for a familiar face, one of my many coping mechanisms, hoping no one would know I am at a Psychologist's office. (God forbid anyone would think I was anything but perfect.)

I will admit that I did not get much out of these weekly therapy sessions. My mindset going in was not positive enough. I later realized that if you don't believe in something, it will have a negative outcome. And that is the key to success; positivity.

After several sessions, I told my mom that I wanted to see someone else. This psychologist was nice but she bugged me more than helped me. Despite not clicking with her, I did learn one very valuable phrase that will forever be in my mental toolbox, "Just Do It." Who knew Nike was such a genius all this time. To me, this simple phrase means you need to stop thinking and just act. If you put action first, the worrying subsides, and the fear is put on the back-burner. When I am put in situations that cause me anxiety, I think of the simple phrase, "Just Do It," and I act. It has become a tool that has saved my worrisome butt too many times.

My mom and I told this psychologist that I was no longer in need of her assistance and we began our search for a new therapist. I was hoping to find someone who was on the younger side, I just was not as comfortable talking to someone who could be my grandmother.

After reading blogs and websites about anxiety, and researching other therapists, we found someone that I thought I could click with. Her name was Megan and she specialized in Cognitive Behavioral Therapy. After doing some research, I felt that this type of therapy would help me the best, finding that it helped many people struggling with anxiety. One positive of seeing her was that her office was located above a Starbucks so I was able to grab a chai before my appointment, and I could fiddle with the lid while I spilled my guts to her.

Megan got me to see things differently. She tried to get to know me before she got to know my anxiety and I think that is what helped me. She saw me for who I am, not my flaw. By our third session I was able to laugh at myself for passing out in Culinary and falling in Biology. I began to really think, "What's the worst that could happen?" about situations that scared me.

Chapter 7

Mental illness is a part of my life. I don't believe I have anything to be ashamed of. Anyone who believes otherwise is the one who does. —Unknown

I continued to struggle throughout my freshman year. Each day had its own speed bump but some were smaller than others. I got by day by day and eventually, the year was over. I did it. I had survived the hardest thing God had thrown at me yet, and the feeling it gave me was indescribable. The feeling of accomplishing something I never thought I could made me realize my true strength. However, that high quickly came back down when I thought, "Wow I have to go through that for three more years!?" I had my mind set on ensuring I would never go back there again.

Chapter 8

How lucky am I to have something that makes saying goodbye so hard.

—Winnie the Pooh

Throughout my four years in high school, I had two boyfriends. The first one was freshman year and I'm not even sure it can be called a relationship. We went to the mall, and the movies, and hung out at my house but we lasted about four months. His parents wouldn't allow me to hang out at their house until they got to know me better. They wanted to take me to dinner but my fear of being in the spotlight, eating in front of them, ordering in front of them, speaking in front of them, got in the way and I refused to go out; leading to the demise of that "relationship." Clearly, it wasn't meant to be.

My second relationship began my sophomore year and lasted almost two years. I learned more about myself in these two years and experienced more personal growth than I thought possible. He was good with words and often filled the awkward silences that I am known to create; I am a girl of few words and I don't care for small talk. One time we were at a football game and he asked me question after question about myself and I did not ask him a single thing back. I would answer and then be quiet. I am surprised he did not give up on me and just walk away that night.

He took me on my first real date to a local bagel shop. I was really anxious, per usual, and didn't have an appetite. I force fed myself a bagel by ripping it into tiny pieces and swallowing them whole; I knew that if I tried to chew them I would just end up gagging and that is the last thing you want to happen on a date. He constantly commented on how quiet I was and I would always respond with how it took a while for me to come out of my shell. He was patient with me, and for the first time in my life, I was able to spend hours with another human being and not get drained from their presence.

I was able to do so much with him which boosted my confidence to a degree I never thought I would reach. There were many firsts for me pushing through my anxiety during this relationship: first time ordering at a drive through with someone else in the car, first time driving someone else other than my dad, first time singing in front of someone, first time crying in front of someone, first time ordering at a restaurant in front of someone; the list could keep going. Needless to say, I was able to be completely myself around him and he still accepted me without judgement. I learned that being me wasn't so bad and that the judgement I saw in everyone was mainly just in my head. That relationship helped me learn to be comfortable in my own skin and taught me that I was my biggest critic and being able to accept yourself and love yourself is the key to personal success.

As most high school relationships do, ours came to an end and I made it a point to stay single for a while. Learning how to be alone helped me grow and become even stronger and happier. I will be grateful for what he did for me because now, my future is looking brighter than ever.

She lost him but she found herself and

somehow that

was everything. —Taylor Swift

SOPHOMORE YEAR

Chapter 9

You gain strength, courage, and confidence by every experience in which you really stop to look fear in the face. You must do the thing which you think you cannot do. —Eleanor Roosevelt

After a horrible summer of failed attempts to convince my parents to let me drop out and do online school, the first day of sophomore year rolled around. I came home from that first day with such a bad migraine. I had been on high alert and anxious for almost 6 hours straight, that certainly has some negative effects on the body.

After a few meltdowns and many tears, my mom and I went to the guidance office to figure out a solution. We ended up creating a 504 plan for me to help accommodate for my anxiety. My teachers, Guidance Counselor, Mom, and I discussed the guidelines of a plan to help me feel less stressed and more able to learn. The teachers and I agreed that they would not call on me out of the blue and would let me take some time to get comfortable in the classroom environment, with hopes that I would eventually feel okay enough to actually raise my hand and participate.

Eventually, everyday got easier and easier to get through. Without the stress of embarrassing myself in front of my classmates, I was actually able to focus on learning. I excelled in all of my classes, keeping my "A" streak and boy, was that a confidence booster.

I slowly came out of my shell and soon I was able to go to sleep and wake up every morning without the feeling of crippling fear. It also helped that I had a boyfriend who was at school which gave me something to look forward to everyday.

"I just have to get through this class and then I can see him." Just a few minutes with him between classes helped to keep my mind from that dark and anxious place before my next class.

For me, incentives were another great tool for my toolbox. On days that I would have to present a project, or on a day I would say something in class, I would reward myself in some way. For example, I would get a chai after school, or maybe have an extra dessert after dinner. Rewards can really help with taking small steps towards a larger goal.

I still struggled and it was a hard year. I still worked on convincing my parents to let me do online school. However, I was able to get through it: taking each moment, each day, one step at a time.

Strength doesn't come from

what you can do, it comes from

overcoming the things you once

thought you couldn't.

—Rikki Rogers,

*I chose this as my senior quote in the yearbook

Chapter 10

Good friends are like stars. You don't always see them, but you know they're always there. —Unknown

Only in movies do people meet on a trip and fall in love. Well, I didn't fall in love but I met a genuine friend on a cruise. Andrew has been my lifeline since we met on an week-long Alaskan Cruise in the summer of 2015. He is someone who learned about who I am from my own point of view and who likes me for my mind, not just my face or my friends. Andrew has gotten to know me better than I know myself. He was there for me whenever I needed a friend or just someone to listen, and I was equally there for him. When I was anxious, he would see the clarity of the situation and give me some ideas on how to fix the problem.

One time, he got in a fight with his parents and "ran" away from home. He called me at midnight in tears as he rode his bike as far from home as he could. Andrew lives in Chicago so I was worried about him being alone on the street that late at night. I just asked him question after question to try to get him to calm down, and he eventually went back home.

Andrew and I are such great friends because we know exactly what the other needs when they need it. When he's sad, I send him videos of cats getting scared of cucumbers. When I'm sad, he tells me how much he cares about me and sends me videos of goats jumping off other goats. He always knows how to make me smile when I need it most.

We may not talk everyday, but when we do, it is like no time has passed. I'm not sure why I got so lucky to get such an amazing friend but I hope the luck never runs out.

Andrew never fails to make my day when a package shows up at my front door with anything from a toy whale to a piece of beautiful jewelry. I'm sure I will always be counting down the days until we meet face to face again, but until then, I know I have a friend to pick me up when I am down.

Having a friend with a fresh set of eyes outside of my own community helped give me perspective into a lot of problems that I faced. He is often my voice of reason and it is nice to have someone to bounce ideas off of who won't be directly affected by a decision that

I make. I truly feel that I would not have improved mentally as much as I did if it weren't for him. I hope everyone can be lucky enough to find themselves a friend like Andy.

Chapter 11

Because of you, I laugh a little harder,

cry a little less, and smile a lot more.

— Unknown

Horses, horses, horses. I know a few people have described me as that "crazy horse girl," but horses make me feel something that people never can. They are truly my addiction. I start to feel lost when I've gone too long without being around a horse. I cannot seem to answer a question in front of my peers but give me a horse and an arena and I'll perform in front of a hundred people. There is only one word to explain it, confidence.

I started riding when I was 4 years old. It was a birthday present from my Nana and Warren. When I first started riding lessons, my feet didn't even pass the saddle, but I loved every minute of it.

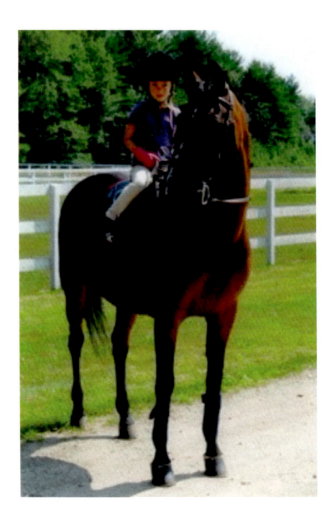

One of my earliest riding memories was when my instructor, Sue, told me to give the horse a hug. Well, she meant with my legs because that is how you hold on, but I bent right over and wrapped my arms around the horse's neck as far as they would go. Everyone got a good laugh out of that one.

After a few years, I moved to a new barn that gave me an immense amount of experience in the horse world. I learned to jump, I went on my first trail ride, I learned how to shave a horse, and I learned a lot of natural horsemanship skills. The biggest thrill however was getting to gallop the horses on the rail trails and on the beach. There is no feeling more freeing. I also became a much more well-rounded rider because I rode a different horse everyday. Each horse was very different so I learned how to adapt to and read each one, which became extremely valuable and helped me gain confidence. I decided that I wanted to focus on a form of riding called dressage so we decided to find a new barn and instructor.

All of the puzzle pieces clicked when my mom and I drove up to Sea Star Stable. We were immediately drawn in by the huge airplane hanger indoor arena, the large outdoor sand arena, and the pasture sprinkled with too many horses to count. It was a sight that took my breath away and gave me butterflies.

I remember stepping out of the car on that first day, whispering, "Mom, look at that pretty black and white horse right there."

I couldn't stop staring. I was mesmerized by this horse. That breathtaking black and white horse, named Jazzie, became my best friend.

Jazzie was a horse that hadn't matched well with too many people because she could be pretty sassy, but she and I clicked immediately. There was something about her that made me feel safe and honestly, unstoppable. Jazzie certainly had her flaws, but I worked my butt off and we became this elegant pair. To me, dressage is a passionate pursuit of perfection and it quickly became my anxiety outlet. I was able to focus on achieving perfection in riding and was able to put less pressure on myself to be perfect outside of the horse world. I was still struggling everyday with being comfortable with myself and wanting to get out of bed everyday but the barn became the space where I could finally "breathe." It was a safe place where I could be myself and worry a whole lot less.

Unfortunately, after three years together, Jazzie got an injury and could no longer be ridden. An extremely loving couple took Jazzie in as a companion for their horse and they love her with their whole hearts. It certainly was not easy, but I knew that she would be in less pain and happy. Plus, if these events did not happen like they did, I never would have met Owen.

***

Kara, my trainer, found Owen in a Facebook ad posted by an old friend of hers. He was the exact opposite of any horse I thought I would want but we went and looked at him anyway. Owen officially became mine in June of 2016, and boy have I learned a lot. I love Owen with every part of me. He makes me happier than I ever thought an animal could. There is nothing like having him lick your cheek or fall asleep with his head on your shoulder. Owen is more experienced than I am so I already knew he was going to teach me things, but I never knew to what degree.

You see, Owen and I are almost too alike. He has anxiety too. Over the past year and a half, I had to put my focus on getting him to trust me so we could work through his fears together. Little did I know, Owen would be curing my fears while I tried to cure his. Learning how to work through those struggles with him led to my own personal growth. I learned how to look at problems from multiple perspectives and that change can only come from action. The lessons Owen taught and continues to teach me are valuable lessons I will use forever.

Owen and I were destined to be together. Ironically, Owen was born on March 18th, 2008; the exact day that my grandfather Warren died. As my bond with Owen strengthens, I feel less and less lost. I truly feel in my heart that Owen has filled the missing

piece of me that Warren took with him when he left.

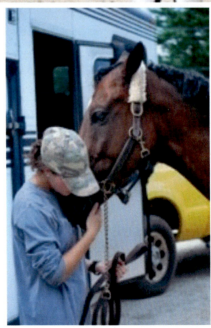

JUNIOR YEAR

Chapter 12

Beauty begins the moment you decide to

be yourself. —Coco Chanel

Junior year was an average year. I went through the motions of going to school, seeing friends, hanging out with my boyfriend, and going to the barn.

My parents finally agreed to let me take one online class with the Virtual Learning and Charter School (VLACS) in place of one class in school. That was when we learned about the Learning Through College Program they offered. If you get accepted into this program you take as many classes as you would like and get dual enrollment credit for them. This means you get both high school and college credit. After talking it through with my parents and guidance counselor, we decided that this would be an amazing opportunity for me to do my junior year.

Since I was enrolled in this program, I became a part-time student at Portsmouth High and a part-time student at VLACS. This meant I only had to go to school for three classes and could then go home and do my online assignments. I am an incredibly motivated person and the online format fit my learning style so I excelled in these online classes. The format of my day also made everything easier on me as I knew that I just had to get through three classes and lunch and then I could go home. There were even days where I did not experience any anxiety at all.

Doing online school is definitely not for everyone. It was a way to help me get through everyday, feel more comfortable at school, and further my education in a new way. Being able to do so well in these online classes also helped some of my school anxiety. I was able to do the video chats with my teacher and answer questions I wasn't prepared for and not go completely blank. I was able to know that it was the fear blocking my brain, not lack of knowledge, when teachers would call on me and I wouldn't know what to say in front of my peers.

Chapter 13

Friends make the good times better and the hard times easier. —Anonymous

I struggled a bit with friends. During my sophomore year, I had eaten lunch with my boyfriend everyday but since he was away at college this year, I didn't have anyone to eat with. I would eat alone in the classroom we ate in last year, or even in the bathroom on the days that teacher had lunch duty. One day a girl named Haley, who was in my American Studies class, walked in to where I was eating alone and basically dragged me down the hall to eat lunch with her friends. I knew a few people in her friend group but I was still super uncomfortable at first. I began eating with them on a regular basis (at Haley's insistence) and spending everyday with the same people quickly led to them becoming close friends. I am very thankful for Haley's actions because she forced me out of my comfort zone and helped me finally feel a sense of belonging.

I now had a strong friend group but I often ditched them to be with my boyfriend every chance I got. That is one of the biggest regrets I have—I catered my life towards him and never got to join in on the experiences my friends got to share. Plus, the more I said no to plans, the fewer times I was being invited; leading to me feeling even more like an outcast.

Friends are the key to finding yourself, loving yourself, accepting yourself, and being happy. Never ever take them for granted.

Chapter 14

"They always say time changes things,

but actually you have to change them

yourself." —Andy Warhol

Junior prom was a night when I surprised

myself the most.

There is this event before prom called "Grand

March." You link arms with your date and walk down

the runway as all the parents cheer, clap and take

pictures; and all your classmates stand on the sidelines

to watch you. I had always told myself that I would not

go to Junior Prom because there was no way in hell that

I was going to do that walk. In my mind, the most probable outcome was that I was going to trip and fall on my face in front of everyone.

Well, when it came down to it, I wanted to go. The thought of participating in Grand March made me want to puke but I was looking forward to wearing that long fancy dress and getting my nails done and putting on a full face of makeup. It was all part of the high school experience and I was not about to let a little fear get in my way.

***

Standing in the hallway outside of the gym, my heart was beating so fast I thought for sure people could actually see it in my chest. Sweat was literally rolling down my sides and I started to get jittery when the

66

music started blaring. We were getting closer and closer to the doors and my nerves were getting worse and worse the closer we got. Before I knew it, it was our turn. We walked through the big arch onto the red carpet and I heard the crowd start cheering. Adrenaline kicked in and I strutted down that carpet. Now what I am about to say even shocks me so prepare yourself; I can easily say that I would do that again any day of the week. I had a blast! The saying is true, "Outside of your comfort zone is where the fun begins."

Chapter 15

Spend your life doing strange things with weird people. — Unknown

Sydney is that friend you make that you never expected to be in your life but one who is never going to leave. I met Sydney when she started riding at my barn. We didn't say much to each other at first but the more we started to talk, the more Sydney came out of her shell, and it wasn't long before we were best friends. I see a lot of myself in Sydney and I think that is how she has helped me. Sydney gets anxious; she doesn't have many friends; she would choose animals over people any day; and she has a weird side that when you see it, you cannot get enough of it. Like me, Sydney understands that people are selfish and cruel.

When Sydney tells me about her day or about something that is bothering her, I see how far I have come. I cannot help but think to myself, "Sydney, I was just like you at the beginning of high school but I'm not like you anymore." Helping Sydney through her problems, has helped me heal some of those same wounds. I am able to tell her that it gets better and truly believe it.

Like me, Sydney found a couple friends (sometimes fewer numbers means stronger bond), and has successfully completed her junior year of high school without dropping out for online school and is ready to find her full potential in her senior year.

Once you learn to make peace with your situation and see the positives in life, nothing is as bad as you make it out to be. Though it may seem like everyone judges you, at the end of the day, the only thing that is important is your opinion of yourself. Look at yourself in the mirror and tell yourself how amazing you are. You may have to do it a million times but when you can look at your reflection and say, "Hey, you're pretty great," you can take on any obstacle that comes your way.

Chapter 16

Fear is the brain's way of saying there is something important for you to overcome. —Rachel Huber

April of my junior year, I started my first "real" job. I sent in an application, created a resume, went in for an interview, and was hired on the spot to work for a local smoothie shop! Now let me tell you, this process was not easy in the slightest. Having to go in for an interview was absolutely terrifying. Being asked "What would you say is your worst quality?" was such a trigger I almost ran out crying. But I held it together because that's what is expected. I thought answering questions about myself would be easy but try answering questions when all you can hear in your head is your heart beating too fast and every part of your body sending off alarms to abort.

As someone who has a hard time throwing away an apple in a classroom out of fear of being looked at, having to take orders, use a register, answer the phone, and make food for someone was mind-boggling. It has taken over a year for me to be able to use the register without visibly shaking. The second I couldn't find the button on the iPad for what smoothie the person wanted my face would turn red and I'd start to sweat. All around it was terrible. After my first day there I went home and bawled my eyes out for hours to my dad saying I couldn't go back there. He made me go back. And honestly, I'm glad he did. Today, I am thriving. I recently just got a raise and was promoted to shift leader. I no longer dread going to work and actually have fun most of the time I'm there.

Everyone has to get a job at some point in their lifetime and I bet most people didn't like every job they had but in order to get through life, you must do things you don't enjoy. I was forced farther outside my comfort zone than I thought I would ever go but it brought me to an even better place. I learned to not be afraid to push yourself because that is where you learn the most and conquer the most.

SENIOR YEAR

Chapter 18

Inhale the future, exhale the past.

— Unknown

I started taking yoga classes at the beginning of my senior year and they have changed my outlook on life. I have been able to explore myself deeper and it has given me tools on how to ground myself when I am in an anxious situation.

After learning and practicing yoga, I am so much more relaxed and am able to stay calm in situations that stressed me out before. I have also noticed a change in my body—I am much more flexible and the practice has helped me gain body confidence. In yoga, you have to trust yourself and your body which has also led to more successes outside of practice.

Yoga has a concept called the Eight Limbs of Yoga. The Eight Limbs were created by Patanjali and they offer guidelines on how to live a meaningful and purposeful life. For example, the first limb called *yama*, deals with ethical standards and sense of integrity, focusing on our behavior and how we conduct ourselves in life. Yamas are universal practices that relate best to what we know as the Golden Rule, "Do unto others as you would have them do unto you." (yogajournal.com). I highly recommend learning about the eight limbs as they have changed my outlook on how to live life and helped me connect to my highest self.

Chapter 19

My best friend is the one who brings out

the best in me. —Henry Ford

My friends are the greatest thing that could've

happened to me. Even though I had ditched them

numerous times to hang out with my boyfriend, they

were immediately there for me when we broke up.

They took me to dinner, the movies, or just to get chai

and talk. I was able to completely throw myself into my

friend group and they didn't bat an eye. That was how I

knew they were true friends.

These girls are so fun to be around no matter the occasion and they never fail to make me laugh. So far this year, we have gone on a hike, to a haunted house, to sports games, to the beach, out to dinner, had game nights, movie nights, a ping-pong tournament, Christmas parties, and so many more fun events. I am thankful for them everyday as they teach me how to live happily.

I have learned that you must stop missing out on life and start saying yes. I missed out on my first few years of high school because I was too busy hiding and succumbing to my fear. Once I started saying yes to my friends, I began to have fun. I began to love my life and love myself. And I must say, it's pretty great having eight smiling faces to support you in everything you do and who you can support right back. These friends are the support system I was missing and I have never been happier or felt more normal. Everyone deserves to have people that make them laugh a little louder, smile a little bigger, and live just a little bit better. I finally found a place where I belong, I finally found the people I belong with.

Chapter 20

Happy are those who take life day by day, complain very little, and are thankful for the little things in life.

— Unknown

Senior year has been my best year yet. I am the happiest I have ever remembered being and I am having so much fun. I truly look forward to everyday. I finished my Learning Through College program on VLACS early in the year. I made the decision to take an additional class in school and that is a decision I never thought I would make. What kid, who has been able to be in school less, would add on another class? The answer is simply because I love it. I look forward to seeing my friends everyday, I look forward to learning, and I look forward to making more accomplishments. Two years ago, I never thought that I would feel this way.

***

Every October, my high school has spirit week. In the past, I didn't want to stand out so I would not dress up too crazily. I always felt, "I don't want to be different, I just want to blend in." Well this year was what showed my biggest change. I went all out every single day of spirit week. I wore face paint, I wore funky clothes, I even went shopping to buy a costume. The pep rally was at the end of the day on a Friday and, as you know, I only stay at school for half days. I hung out at school in my costume just so I could scream my head off and have a blast in the gym with all my peers.

It was in that moment of craziness during the pep rally that I came to realize how much I was going to miss this school and the people around me. I had always been counting down the days until graduation but now, that will be quite the bittersweet day.

***

I now have this motto, "Do one thing a day that scares you." When you can push yourself and accomplish something you never thought you could, you come one step closer to becoming your highest self. Plus, there is no better feeling than facing a fear successfully, so why not get that high everyday?

I constantly see how much I've changed. In fact, tomorrow is the beginning of a new quarter at school and I feel no anxiety. If that isn't success, then I don't know what is.

Chapter 21

Sometimes you will never know the value

of a moment until it becomes a memory.

— Dr. Seuss

I often found peace in music so here are some songs that I highly recommend to those fighting their own battles.

- Praying—Kesha
- Where it all begins—Hunter Hayes
- Anxiety—Trey Schafer (E)
- Reason to Hope—Ron Pope
- Silence—Marshmello, Khalid
- Girl America—Matt Kearney
- I Fall Apart—Post Malone (E)
- Tomorrow Never Comes—Zac Brown
- We All Die Trying To Get It Right—Vance Joy
- I Get Overwhelmed—Dark Room (E)
- 1-800-273-8255—Logic
- Heal—Tom Odell
- Punchin' Bag—Cage The Elephant

- Trouble—Coldplay
- 19th Nervous Breakdown—The Rolling Stones
- The Climb—Miley Cyrus
- Where Is My Mind—Nada Surf
- Sideways—Citizen Cope
- The Meadows—Dear Seattle (E)
- I don't wanna be sad—Simple Plan
- What If—Adam Friedman
- Mind Over Matter—Pvris
- Tennyson—Adam Barnes
- Paralyzed—NF
- Sad Song—Scotty Sire
- The Fear—Ben Howard
- Heavydirtysoul—Twenty One Pilots
- Drown—Seafret
- I'm Losing Friends—Tanner Swift
- Stone Cold—Demi Lovato
- Forget The Lies—Quietdrive
- Warrior—Demi Lovato
- Even Then—Lizzy Cameron
- You're Not Alone—Owl City
- Broken—Lund (E)
- Afraid—The Neighborhood
- Nobody Knows—The Lumineers
- Breaking Inside—Shinedown
- Ode To Sleep—Twenty One Pilots
- Nobody Knows—Pink
- Migraine—Twenty One Pilots
- Rainy Season—Hunter Hayes
- Goner—Twenty One Pilots
- the lonely—Christina Perry
- Keep Your Head Up—Ben Howard
- How To Save a Life—The Fray

What I've learned:

- Surround yourself with people who know your worth and show you the love you deserve

- Find a hobby/passion that you love with your whole heart

- Choose your friends wisely

- Learn to love and accept yourself

- Appreciate what you get out of failure

- Find confidence

- Always look for the positive

- Ask yourself "What's the worst that could happen?"

- Music can take away the lonely and make you feel any emotion you want

- Journal, it is never good to keep those thoughts to yourself

- Exercise can be a savior

- Never be afraid to ask for help

- Stand up for what you believe in

- You are never as alone as you feel

- Do one thing a day that scares you

One of the most cleansing things I do is journal, but sometimes it can be hard to think of something to write about. Some days I just do a "mind dump;" just writing anything and everything that comes to mind. Other days though, I look through pre-prompted journals to retrieve my thoughts. Here are a few prompts for you to connect with:

My goal for today is:

_____

_____

_____

I love:

_____

_____

_____

_____

Who loves me:

_____

_____

_____

_____

What made me thankful today:

_____

_____

_____

What made me smile today:

_____

_____

_____

Smile at a stranger, what happened?

_____

_____

What I accomplished today:

_____

_____

_____

_____

What I did today that scared me:

_____

_____

_____

_____

How did someone else make you happy today?

_____

_____

_____

Imperfection I overlooked today:

_____

_____

_____

Epilogue

This anxiety will always be part of me. It isn't something that just goes away, however I have learned to live with it and be successful. I will never be able to do some things the easy way, but I know that I will be just fine. High school has tested me and caused me to fall, but also to soar. College is just around the corner and I am scared but excited to conquer the new challenges it throws my way.

My final advice to you is stop running from your monster. Look it in the eye, stand strong, and persevere. You never know what you can accomplish outside of your comfort zone and past your fear, but never be afraid to ask for help. Sometimes, the monster is too strong to conquer on your own.

Good luck, I believe in you.

Life is short. Stop worrying about what might happen. Live in the moment. Follow your dreams. Be with good people. Forget what hurt you— but never forget what it taught you. —Karen Salmansohn

83425453R00055

Made in the USA
Middletown, DE
11 August 2018